Brown Bear, Brown Bear
by Bill Martin, Jr.
Holt, Rinehart & Winston 1967

1

READ

Read *Brown Bear, Brown Bear* for fun. You will find that most children will memorize this story in a very short time and will enjoy reciting it with you.

Read *Brown Bear, Brown Bear.*

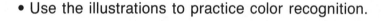

2

READ IT AGAIN

• Use the illustrations to practice color recognition.

Ask "What color is the _____?" "Can you see anything around you that is the same color?" "Can you think of another animal that is the same color?"

• "What do you see?" (A variation of "I Spy.")

Have the children look around the classroom. Then call on someone, asking " (child's name) , (child's name) , what do you see?" Child answers, "I see a (color) (object) close to me."

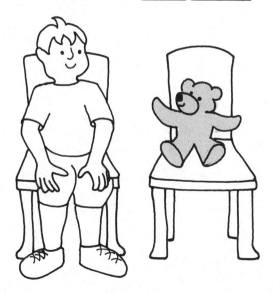

1

3

READ IT AGAIN

Read *Brown Bear, Brown Bear.*

• Reproduce the pictures on page 5 on several colors of construction paper. (You may want to laminate the pictures as they will be handled by the children. This will make them last longer.) Cut the cards apart. These cards can be used in several ways.

Have children sit in a circle. Place the animal cards in the middle of the circle. Give the color and name of one animal. Select a child to find that animal card. Continue until all of the cards have been picked up. You may stop at this point if children are just learning to recognize colors or continue by doing one of the following:

Have each child turn to his neighbor, show the card, and ask "What do you see?"

Have children group themselves by color (all of the reds) or by animals (all of the bears). This is noisy, but it's a fun way to practice categorization.

Ask children to return the cards to you by saying "Please give me all of the (blue cats) ."

Ask riddles such as "This animal can swim and is the color of grass." The children with green fish give their cards to the teacher.

• Use the same cards to play "Go Fish" or "Concentration" in groups of two or four.

Other Activities

Math

- Beginning Graphing:

  Create a simple graph based on animal preference. Provide sufficient cards (using the patterns on page 5) for each child to select a picture of the animal they prefer (bear, fish, duck, or cat). Each child then places the picture in the correct place on the graph.

| cat | fish | duck | bear |

  When the graph is complete, have children count each column to see how many of each animal were selected. Ask questions such as ''Which animal did the most people choose?'' or ''Did the most people pick the bear or the duck?'' With older students you can also ask questions such as ''How many more people picked the cat than picked the duck?''

- Patterning:

  Make several copies of the cards on page 5. Use two or more of the animals to create patterns. Begin with short, simple patterns such as bear, cat, bear, cat, etc. Provide longer, more complex patterns as children become more experienced with patterning.

  Select one or more children to copy your pattern.
  Select one or more children to continue the pattern.
  Show the pattern, remove it, and have children try to recreate it from memory.

- Counting:

  Use the same set of cards for counting experiences. Display several animals of the same kind. Ask children questions such as ''How many _____ do you see?'' ''Can you give me the same number of _____?'' ''If I take one _____ away, how many will I have left?''

Language

- Take a "seeing walk" around the schoolyard or neighborhood.

Have children see how many things they can find that are a specific color. For example, you might be looking for everything you can find that is green. When a child sees something, stop and discuss it with the group. When you return to the classroom, record the results of the walk in some way. For example:

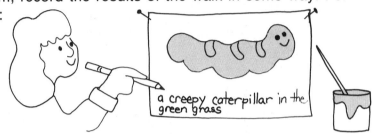

a creepy caterpillar in the green grass

Allow each child to name something green that was seen on the walk. Make a large chart listing these items. Find a picture (or draw one) to put next to each word so you have the beginning of a color "pictionary" that children can refer to in the future.

Let each child that went on the walk paint a large picture of something green that he or she saw. Write a short phrase about the picture on the painted paper (green grass, green car, etc.) and put the pictures up around the room.

- Dictate or write sentences.

Let each child copy the question. Then illustrate the answer to create a page for a group or class book. For example:

Mother! Mother! What do you see?
Santa! Santa! What do you see?
Lady Bug! Lady Bug! What do you see?

I see a funny dog Looking at me!

Staple the finished pages in a cover made of construction paper or colored tag. Children love to "read" each other's stories.

Note: First graders or more advanced Kindergarten children may be ready to write their answer as well as draw it.

Reproduce this page on several colors of construction paper. The cards will last longer if they are laminated or covered with clear Contact paper.

> *Corduroy*
> by Don Freeman
> Puffin Books 1968

1 READ

Read *Corduroy* for fun.

2 READ IT AGAIN

Read *Corduroy*.

- Ask questions such as these:
  Where did Corduroy live?
  Why wouldn't Mother let Lisa buy Corduroy?
  What did Corduroy go looking for?
  How did Corduroy finally get a button?

- "What is it called?"
  Use the illustrations to develop new vocabulary and to practice oral language skills. Ask questions about the pictures. For example:
  Can you name the toys on this page?
  What is the man doing?
  Why do you think that girl looks sad?
  What is this piece of furniture called?
  What is this _____ used for?

- Practice story sequencing. Ask "What happened first in the story?" and "What happened next?" If children have difficulty, be more specific. "What happened after the night watchman found Corduroy?" Use the illustrations to help children when they experience difficulty.

3
READ IT AGAIN

Read *Corduroy.*

Have a day for everyone to bring their favorite toy animal. (Don't forget to bring yours!) Plan a day of activities around the toy animals. For example:

• Toy Animal Day — Language

Plan time for children to tell about their animals. Encourage the use of complete sentences.

Use the animals to encourage careful listening. Place several of the toy animals on a table. Ask a riddle about one of the animals. See who can find the animal you are describing.

Have animal crackers at snack time. Name the animals and their parts as children nibble.

• Toy Animal Day — Math

Put all of the toy animals in the middle of the rug. Have children sort them into categories, then count how many there are in each set. Ask questions such as "How many __(teddy bears)__ are there?" or "Are there more __(cats)__ or more __elephants__?"

Arrange some of the toy animals in a row. This may be done in a random manner or by size. Use the animals to practice ordinal numbers. Ask "Which animal is first in line?" "Is the __(bear)__ first or last in line?" "Which animal is third in line?" If the animals are arranged by size, ask comparison questions. "Which animal is the largest?" "Which animal is smaller than the __(lion)__?"

Read *Corduroy.*

- Categories — Bring a collection of buttons of different sizes and colors to class. (Or reproduce the button patterns on page 9 on tag. This is safer for children younger than five. Color the buttons with felt marking pens.) Have children sort the buttons by size, by color, or by the number of holes in the buttons.

- Counting — Count how many buttons you have altogether. Count how many buttons you have of each size and of each color.

- Graphing — Glue each color of button in columns on a large chart to create a simple bar graph.

Other Activities

Language — Take a field trip to a department store. See if you can find one with an escalator and an elevator. (Be sure you have adequate adult help. This is necessary for the children's safety and for your sanity!)

"How are escalators and stairs alike/different?"
"How are an elevator and an escalator alike/different?"

Art — Run the button patterns (on page 9) on various colors of construction paper. (Or use real buttons with older students.) Have children create button pictures. The pictures can be designs created from the buttons, or pictures where the button is a part of a drawn or painted picture.

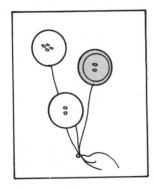
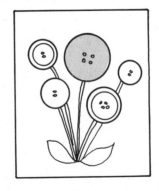
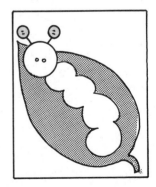

Run these buttons on colored construction paper or on tag.

Buttons, Buttons, Buttons

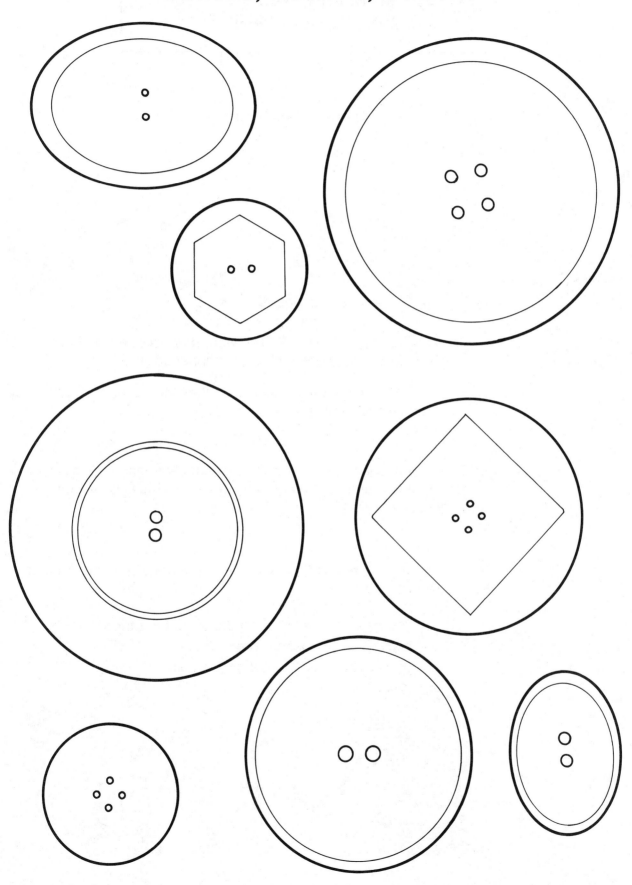

> # *If You Give a Mouse a Cookie*
> ## by Laura Joffe Numeroff
> ## Harper & Row 1985

1 READ

Read *If You Give a Mouse a Cookie* for fun.

2 READ IT AGAIN

Read *If You Give a Mouse a Cookie.*

- "What will happen next?" — Tell what has occurred and ask your students to respond with what happened next.

    "I gave my mouse a cookie. What will happen next?" ("He will want a glass of milk.")

- Show each illustration. Have children practice language skills by naming items and actions in the pictures and looking for the humorous elements.

- "Use your imagination!" — Ask your students to try and think of what might happen if...

    you gave an elephant a peanut butter sandwich.
    you gave a chicken a grain of corn.
    you gave a child an ice cream cone.

READ IT AGAIN

Read *If You Give a Mouse a Cookie.*

- The Merry Mouse — Use this game to practice the sound the letter "m" makes.

Make stick puppets using the pattern on page 12 and tongue depressors. Have the children use their mice to complete this sentence about words which begin (or end) with the "m" sound.

"My merry mouse likes milk."
"My merry mouse likes muffins."
"My merry mouse likes mud."

- "Where's the Mouse?" — Use the same stick puppets to practice positional words.

The children ask "Where's the mouse?" The teacher replies by giving a location. The children hold their stick puppets in the place named by the teacher. For example:

"He is over your head."
"He is behind your back."
"He is under your chin."
"He is between your legs."

Use places such as these for children who are ready for left-right practice.

"He is in your left hand."
"He is over your right shoe."

Note: Reproduce this page on white construction paper or tag. Color and cut out the puppet. Glue or tape it to a tongue depressor.

Merry Mouse
Stick Puppet

> ## Inch by Inch
> ### by Leo Lionni
> ### Astor-Honor, Inc. 1960

READ

Read *Inch by Inch* for fun.

READ IT AGAIN

Read *Inch by Inch*.

- Ask questions such as these:

    What was the robin going to do to the inchworm?
    What could the inchworm do?
    What kinds of animals did the inchworm measure?
    How did the inchworm escape from the nightingale?
    Can you think of a way to measure how long a song is?

- Use the illustrations to help children recall the names of the birds in the story.

    Brainstorm to list all of the kinds of birds the children can name. Older children may be ready to take the list of birds and group them into categories such as big birds and little birds, birds that cannot fly, birds we keep as pets, etc.

    Get picture books of birds from the library to share with your class.

Read It Again

Read *Inch by Inch.*

This is a good story to use as you introduce linear measurement to children. Use the inchworm pattern on page 16 with the following activities.

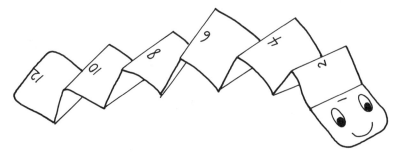

- Use the inchworm to find the answer to questions such as:

"Is your foot longer or shorter than your inchworm?"
"About how many inchworms long is this table?"
"Can you find something in our classroom that is about three inchworms long?"

- Use the inchworms to begin inch measurement with older students. The inchworm is twelve inches long from the tip of the nose to the tip of the tail. Each body segment is one inch long. Let children measure all sorts of items in the classroom and on each other. Have several children measure the same item to see if they come up with the same answer.

- "How big are our feet?"

Have children measure one of their feet. Graph the results to find out the answer to questions such as:

"Who has the longest feet in class?"
"Who has the shortest feet in class?"
"How many people have feet that are about 5 inches long?"

Science — "What is a bird?"

Lead children in a discussion to determine the main characteristics of a bird. You may want to list these on a chart to create a class story.

Compare and contrast the inchworm and a bird. Help children to decide how the two animals are alike and how they are different.

Art

- Study the illustrations by Lionni. See if the children can decide what he used to make his pictures. Explain that this type of illustration is called a collage. Let them make their own bird collages from cut or torn pieces of paper. Add details and texture with crayons. Display these around the classroom.

- Create a grass "jungle" from a variety of green wallpaper or wrapping paper samples. (Let each child make several leaves and blades of grass.) Put these on a bulletin board and add shiny green inchworms cut from green foil paper. Add other creatures that might live in the grass if you wish.

Reproduce this pattern on green construction paper or on tag.

Inchworm

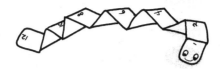

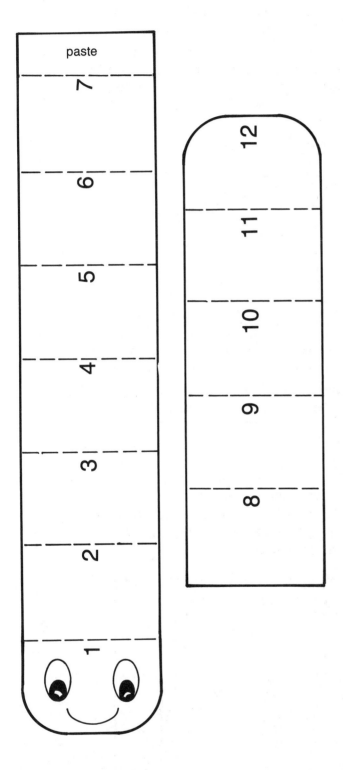

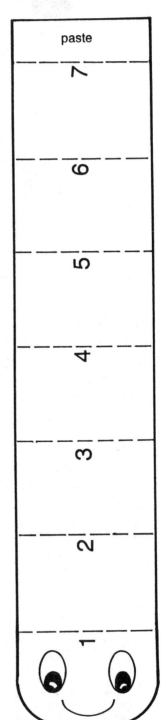

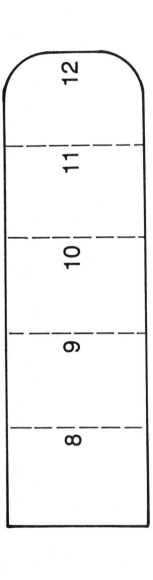

Read It Again

> # *Moon Bear*
> ## by Frank Asch
> ## Charles Scribner's Sons 1978

READ

Read *Moon Bear* for fun.

READ IT AGAIN

Read *Moon Bear*.

- Ask questions such as:

    What did Bear think was happening to the moon?
    What did he start doing to fatten up the moon?
    What really happened to the honey?
    Why was Bear getting thinner?
    Why was Bear feeling sad?

- Have a "honey tasting" party.

    See if you can find honey in the comb, so your students can see how bees "package" the honey they make. *Bees and Honey* published by Oxford Scientific Films has large, clear photographs of bees and the inside of their hive for students that show an interest in knowing more about bees and how they make honey.

- Phases of the Moon

    Reproduce the patterns on page 20 on white construction paper. You will need to make the two slits that are required. Have children color the moon pictures yellow and the other areas black. (If this is too difficult for your students, make one or more samples yourself and place the activity in a center for children to share.)

3
READ IT AGAIN

Read *Moon Bear.*

- "Moon" Rubbings

  Each child will need a sheet of white construction paper and a piece of yellow crayon (without its wrapping). Take a small group at a time out onto a blacktop or rough sidewalk area. Have them lay the paper on the blacktop and make a large yellow circle using the side of the crayon. (You may need to provide a large circle template for younger students to trace.) The rough surface creates the moon's "craters." Then have children paint over their moon pictures with a wash made of black tempera paint diluted with water. This creates the night sky. After the paint has dried, add shiny, stick-on stars to complete the look of the night sky.

- Make "moon" cookies.

  Cooking with children is a wonderful opportunity to develop language, to practice measurement skills, and encourage cooperation.

  Follow your favorite sugar cookie recipe. Have plenty of round cookie cutters available. Very young children can observe as you mix the dough. They can cut out one or more cookies with your help. Older students will be able to help measure, stir, roll out the dough, etc. Frost completed cookies with pale yellow frosting to represent the full moon. Cut some cookies to represent other phases of the moon.

  Enjoy the cookies with milk later in the day. You may want to re-read *Moon Bear* to the children as they enjoy their "moon" cookies.

Language

- "What's in Bear's Bowl?"

Practice the sound of the letter "b" using the patterns on page 21. Explain that Bear's bowl will only hold things that have a "b" sound. Use the objects on the bottom of this page (or cut "b" pictures from magazines) to practice the sound. Place one object at a time in the bowl and have children tell what they see. Then ask "Can you think of anything else that can go in Bear's bowl?"

- Make a "B" book.

Use the same bear pattern to make a little shape book of "b" pictures or words. Run two bears on brown construction paper for the cover. Make bears on white paper for the pages. Have children draw or find pictures of "b" objects. Add the word if you wish. Put all the pages together and staple into the brown bear cover.

Reproduce on construction paper (or make from felt or Pellon).

Reproduce this page on white construction paper. Make the two slits with a mat knife or Exacto blade.

pull

The Phases of the Moon

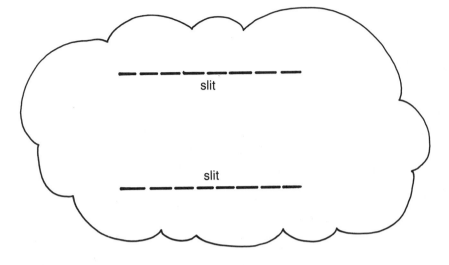

slit

slit

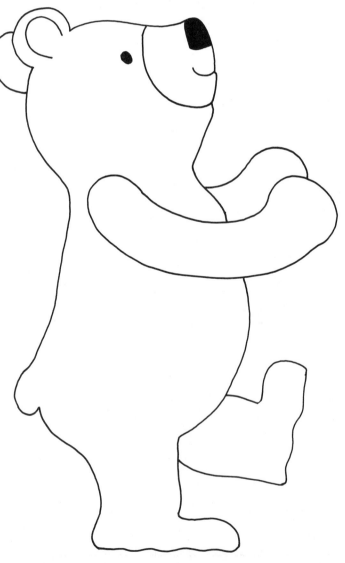

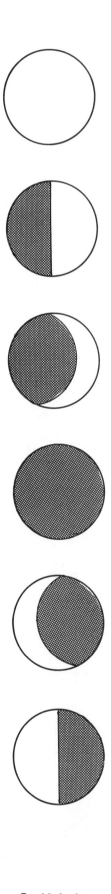

20

Reproduce these patterns on white construction paper. Color the bear brown. (Make the patterns from felt or Pellon to use on a flannel board.)

What's in Bear's bowl?

> # Peter's Chair
> ## by Ezra Jack Keats
> ## Harper & Row 1967

READ

Read *Peter's Chair* for fun.

READ IT AGAIN

Read *Peter's Chair.*

- Ask questions such as these:
  Why had Father painted all of Peter's old furniture pink?
  Did Peter like his new sister?
  Why did Peter want to run away?
  What did he take with him?
  Why did Peter come back into the house?
  How did Peter trick his mother?

- Talk about younger brothers and sisters. Younger children may need help getting started. You might ask questions such as "Do you have a baby at your house?" "What does your baby do that you like/don't like?" "How do you help with the baby?"

READ IT AGAIN

Read *Peter's Chair.*

- Use the illustrations to help children recall events in the story. As you show each picture, select a child to explain what is happening in that part of the story. Then, if you have older students, close the book and have them try to tell the story in order. (You may even want to write their version on a large chart.)

- Use the illustrations to talk about different ways pictures are made for books. Show each picture and help children to determine which parts were made from wallpaper, doilies, etc. and which parts are drawn or painted. (This will be difficult for really young children.)
  Provide large sheets of wallpaper samples for the children to paint on. Older children may want to try making a picture. Younger children can paint designs or do sponge printing on their samples.

4

READ IT AGAIN

Read *Peter's Chair.*

- Several pieces of furniture are named in this story. Have children see how many different kinds of furniture they can name. It is helpful to have magazines and catalogs on hand for motivation and to help children learn to recognize all of the types being named.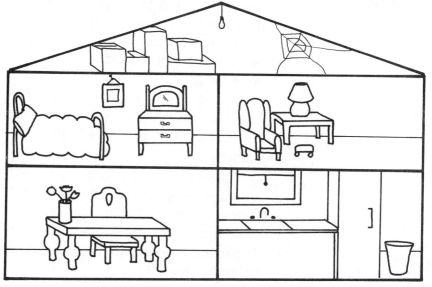

- Cut many pictures of furniture out of magazines, catalogs, and newspaper ads. (Let children who know how to use scissors help you.) The pictures can be used in various ways.

Have a group of children sit in a circle with the teacher or a helper. Put all of the pictures in the middle of the circle with the picture side down. Go around the circle letting each child pick up a picture, turn it over, and say its name. If the child is correct, he keeps the picture. If he is incorrect, say the name of the item and have it returned to the center of the circle to be picked again later.

Have the children determine which items go in a stated category.

Which pictures show furniture that belongs in the bedroom?
Which pictures show furniture you can sit on?
Which pictures show furniture that is made of wood?

Or have children put pictures into categories that they develop. A child might pick up three items because they are all red, they are all big, they are all soft, etc.

Read It Again

> ## Spiders in the Fruit Cellar
> ### by Barbara M. Joosse
> ### Alfred A. Knopf 1983

1 READ

Read *Spiders in the Fruit Cellar* for fun.

2 READ IT AGAIN

Read *Spiders in the Fruit Cellar.*

- Ask questions such as:
  Who is this story about?
  What did Elizabeth's mother want her to do?
  Where was the jar of peaches?
  Why was Elizabeth afraid to go down in the fruit cellar?
  What happened when she did go?
  How did her mother make Elizabeth feel better?

- In the Fruit Cellar
  Many children have never lived in a house with a cellar. Explain to your students where a cellar (or basement) is located in a house. Have children see if they can recall what was in the cellar of Elizabeth's house. Then allow time to discuss what other things might be kept in a cellar (or basement).

3 READ IT AGAIN

Read *Spiders in the Fruit Cellar.*

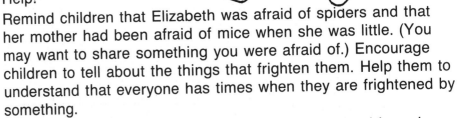

- Help!
  Remind children that Elizabeth was afraid of spiders and that her mother had been afraid of mice when she was little. (You may want to share something you were afraid of.) Encourage children to tell about the things that frighten them. Help them to understand that everyone has times when they are frightened by something.
  See if they can recall how Elizabeth's mother helped her when Elizabeth said she was afraid of spiders. Ask how other people help them when they are frightened.

- Spiders
  Use the patterns on page 26 to teach your students the parts of a spider. Make the pieces out of felt or Pellon to use on a flannel board. Cut from tag, color, and laminate or cover with clear Contact paper to use as a puzzle in a center.
  The same pieces can become an individual cut-and-paste puzzle for older students.

Read *Spiders in the Fruit Cellar.*

Use the patterns on page 27 to practice math skills. Reproduce them on felt or Pellon to use on a flannel board. Make them out of tag to use on a table or rug with a small group of children.

Practice counting skills:

Put the jar on the flannel board. Place a number of peaches on the jar. Ask ''How many peaches are in my jar?'' Select a child to count the peaches. Repeat with different amounts of peaches.

Select a child to put a stated number of peaches on the jar.

Put a felt numeral on the jar. Select a child to place that amount of peaches on the jar.

More than/Less than:

Put several peaches on the jar. Ask ''How many peaches will be on the jar if I take one away?'' or ''How many peaches will be on the jar if I add one more?''

Put up two jars. Put different numbers of peaches on each jar. Ask ''Which jar has the most/fewest peaches?'' If your students have difficulty, have them match the peaches one to one using strips of yarn.

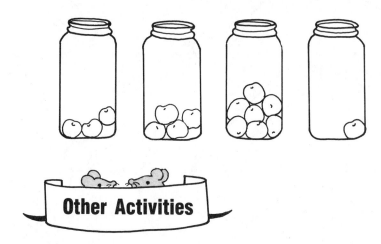

Other Activities

Language — Have your students name all of the types of fruit they can remember. Let them find as many different kinds of fruit as they can from magazines and grocery ads.

Eat-a-peach Day — Eat canned peaches at snack time. Explain to older children why fruit is put into jars or cans. If fresh peaches are available, have children compare the taste, smell, and texture of the fresh and canned peaches.

Copy these pieces on felt or Pellon for use on a flannel board or on tag to use as a puzzle in a center.

Spider

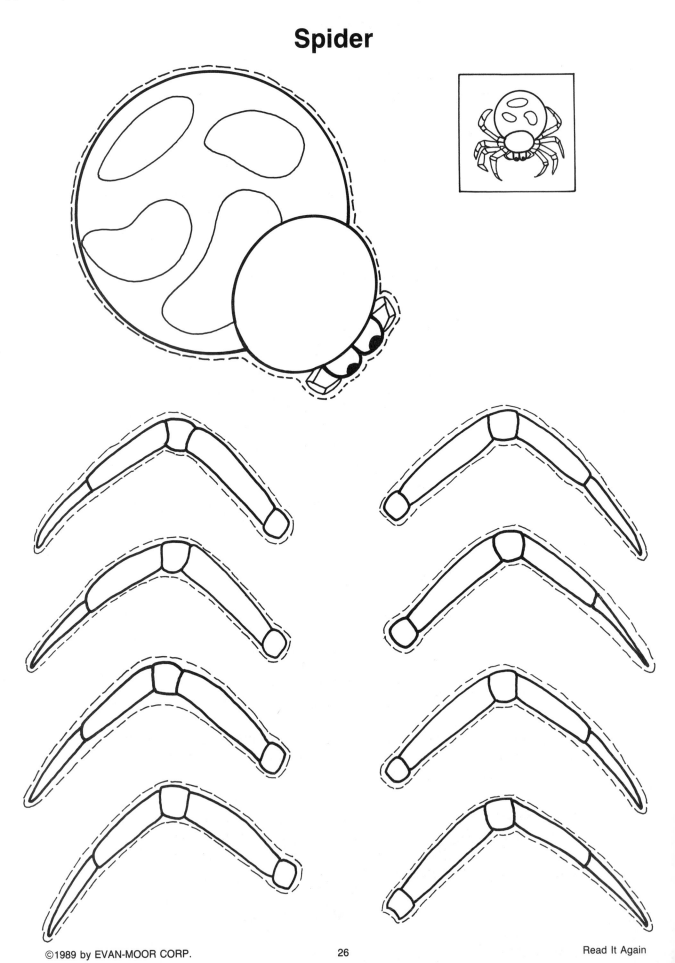

26

Read It Again

How many peaches are in my jar?

Read It Again

> # *The April Rabbits*
> ## by David Cleveland
> ## Coward, McCann & Geoghegan 1978

1 READ

Read *The April Rabbits* for fun.

2 READ IT AGAIN

Read *The April Rabbits.*

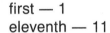

- Ask questions such as these:
  What animal followed Robert home?
  What did the rabbits do in this story?
  How many rabbits did Robert see on the _____ day?

first — 1	twenty-third — 23
eleventh — 11	last day — 0

  How do you think Robert felt when he saw all of those rabbits? (Was he scared, curious, amused, etc.?)
  What do you think will happen with the hippopotamus?

- Real or Make-Believe?
  Show each illustration to your students. Have them determine if a real rabbit could do that action or if it is make-believe.

3 READ IT AGAIN

Read *The April Rabbits.*

It is fun to wear rabbit ears while doing the following activities. Reproduce the pattern on page 30 on white construction paper to create rabbit ear headbands for your students to wear.

- Act it out!
  There are many action words in this story. Have children show you how they think a rabbit would...

nibble a carrot	look scared	fly
tap-dance	march in a line	take a nap
sing	drink a soda	take a bath
dig a hole	ride a skateboard	read a book

- Let's Follow Robert
  Choose one child to be "Robert." All of the other children are the April rabbits and must follow along as "Robert" leads them in a game of "Follow the Leader." (The teacher may need to be the leader if the class is very young.)

 Read It Again

READ IT AGAIN

Read *The April Rabbits.*

There are many math readiness activities you can do with this story. Reproduce the rabbit patterns on page 31 on several colors of construction paper to use with these activities.

- Counting — Decide how high you want to practice counting. Select that many rabbits.

    Have your students count the rabbits as you pin them on a bulletin board or place them on a table.

    Remove one or more rabbits. Ask "How many rabbits do you see now?" (Repeat several times.)

    Remove all of the rabbits. Select a child to show you a stated number of rabbits. (Repeat several times.)

- Use the story to talk about calendars. Explain how a whole month passes as the story progresses. Use a real calendar face. Touch each day of the month and ask children to tell you how many rabbits Robert saw on that day.

Other Activities

Language — "Use your imagination!"
Robert had rabbits following him home for a full month. Then he saw a hippopotamus. Can you think of an interesting animal that might follow you home? What kinds of things could it do?

Rabbits did many funny things in this book. Can you think of even more funny or unusual activities make-believe rabbits might do?

Art — Paint big rabbits using white, brown, or black paint. When the rabbits are dry, cut them out and add cotton balls for fluffy tails. If you can find room, pin these rabbits up in a row. You may even want to have someone paint a hippo to add to the end of the parade of rabbits.

Note: Reproduce this page on white or light brown construction paper. Cut out the headband. Glue or staple a 2½'' (3.3 cm) by 11'' (28 cm) strip of paper to the rabbit. Fit it to the child's head and staple it together to form rabbit ears.

Rabbit Ear Headband

Rabbits Everywhere!

Read It Again

1 READ

Read *The Mystery of the Missing Red Mitten* for fun.

2 READ IT AGAIN

Read *The Mystery of the Missing Red Mitten.*

- Ask questions such as these:
  What has Annie lost?
  Where did Annie look for her lost mitten?
  Why do you think Annie keeps losing mittens?
  How do you think her mother feels about all of those lost mittens?
  Do you think she will lose any more mittens this winter? Why or why not?

- Use your imagination!

  Reproduce the mitten pattern on page 35 on red construction paper. Say "Annie has a great imagination. What did she imagine the mouse could do with her mitten? What did she think would grow if she planted her other mitten? How do you think the mitten could be used?" Let each child hold a "red mitten" while explaining how it could be used.

  The same mittens may be used for beginning story writing. Have each child dictate a use for the mitten. Write the story on the red mitten and let the child take it home to share with family members.

3 READ IT AGAIN

Read *The Mystery of the Missing Red Mitten.*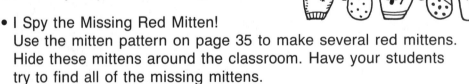

- I Spy the Missing Red Mitten!
  Use the mitten pattern on page 35 to make several red mittens. Hide these mittens around the classroom. Have your students try to find all of the missing mittens.

- Big Red
  Provide large sheets of paper and several shades of red paint. Encourage your students to paint something big (real or imaginary) that can be red. When the paintings are dry, provide time for each child to tell about his big, red picture.

READ IT AGAIN

Read *The Mystery of the Missing Red Mitten.*

- Review the part of the story that explains how the mitten was found.
- Let each child recreate the snowman with the missing red mitten. Reproduce the pattern on page 36 on white construction paper.

Students color the snowman.

Give each student a 1¼'' (4 cm) square of white construction paper. Fold down a flap on one side.

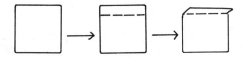

Paste the folded portion of the square so the flap covers snowman's heart.

By lifting the flap, students can see the heart.

Other Activities

Language — Teach your students the poem "The Mitten Song" by Marie Louise Allen.

You may want to put the poem on a chart for older students to see as you say the poem. After a few repetitions, children will have memorized the poem. Many will begin to recognize words that are used frequently in the poem.

Thumbs in the . . .
Fingers all . . .

Math — Practice patterning.

Reproduce the mitten on page 35 in several different colors. Make enough mittens so you can build a pattern and have one or more students recreate it. (Older or more able students can continue a pattern started by the teacher.)

Art — Give each child a copy of the mitten on page 35. They can create designs on their mittens using crayons, paint, or sponge printing. (You may want to spend some time discussing different types of patterns before they begin.)

Mitten Pattern

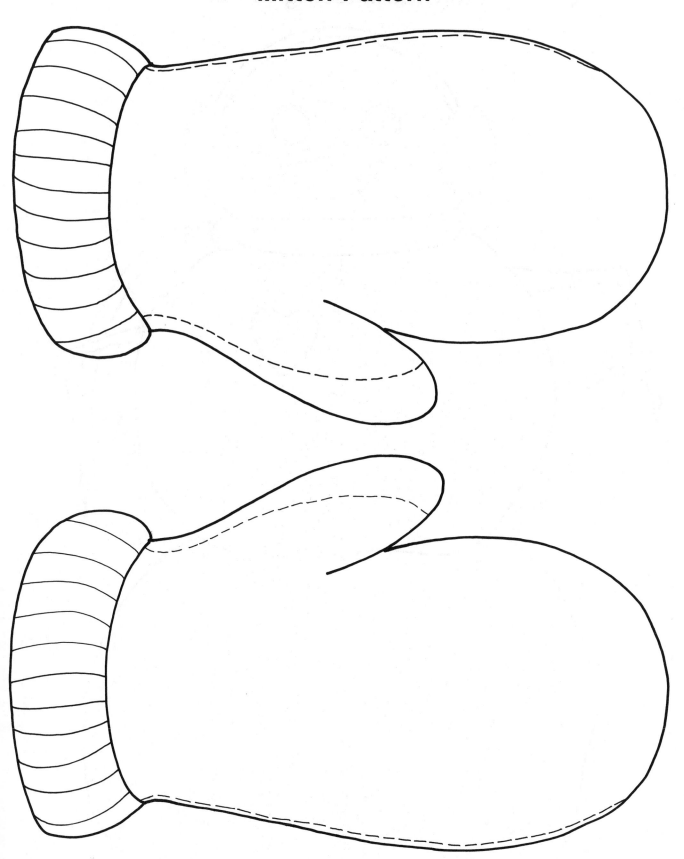

Find the Missing Mitten

Read It Again

> # The Napping House
> ## by Audrey Wood
> ### Harcourt Brace Jovanovich 1984

1 READ

Read *The Napping House* for fun. Many children will be able to learn the repetitive parts of this story.

2 READ IT AGAIN

Read *The Napping House.*

- **Flannel Board Story**

  Reproduce the patterns on pages 39 and 40. Make them out of felt or Pellon to use on a flannel board (or cut them out of construction paper to use as silhouettes with an overhead projector).

  Let the children assist you by putting up the correct pieces as you read the story.

- **Sequencing**

  Use the same story pieces. Select one or more children to put the characters into the correct order on the bed. (You can run these pieces on paper and let older students color, cut, and paste the pieces onto another sheet for sequencing practice.)

3 READ IT AGAIN

Read *The Napping House.* Use the illustrations in one of the ways described below.

- Open the book to the page showing Granny in bed and the child in the chair. See if the children can find all six characters that are in the story.

  Go through the pages and observe how each character moves in each new picture.

- Share the pictures and observe how the colors change as the rainy day becomes a sunny day as the "nappers" begin to wake up.

  Let children paint either a rainy day picture or a sunny day picture. Display the finished paintings, grouping each type together.

Language Development — This story is full of wonderful descriptive language. Take time to talk about all of the words that are used for the sleeping characters (snoozing, dozing, dreaming, etc.) and for the actions that occur after the flea takes a bite (scares, claws, bumps, etc.).

Memory — Begin a refrain and see if the children can complete it with the correct animal. For example, "A wakeful _____."

Comparisons — Use the characters in this story to practice size words such as large, larger, largest; small, smaller, smallest; big, bigger, biggest.

Positional Words — Use the characters stacked on the bed to practice positional words. Ask questions such as:

    "Who is on top?"
    "Who is on the bottom?"
    "Who is between the _____ and the _____?"

Read It Again

The Napping House

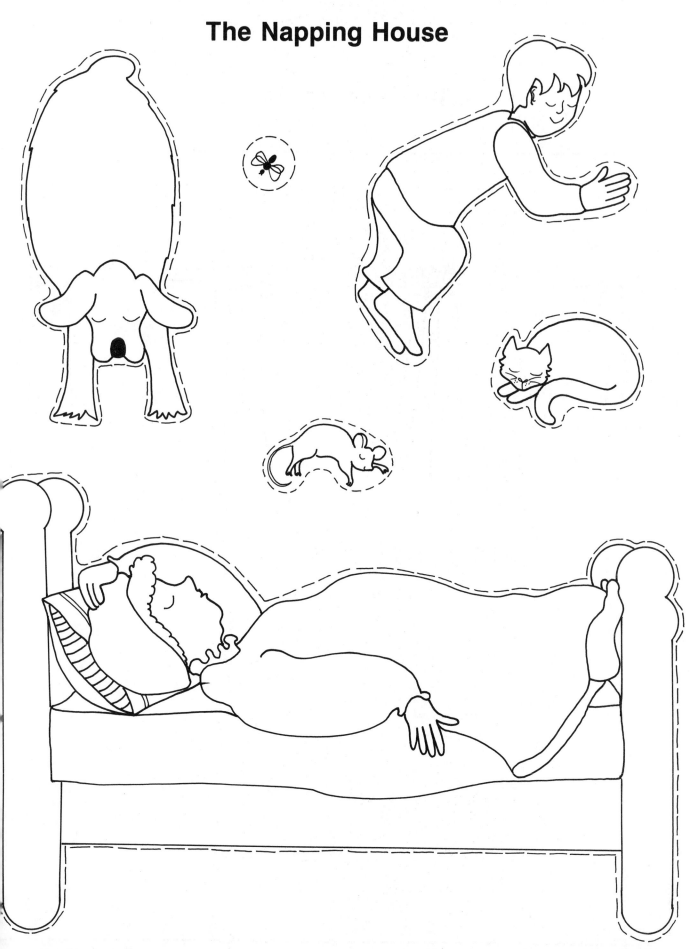

Read It Again

Reproduce this pattern on felt or Pellon to use on a flannel board.

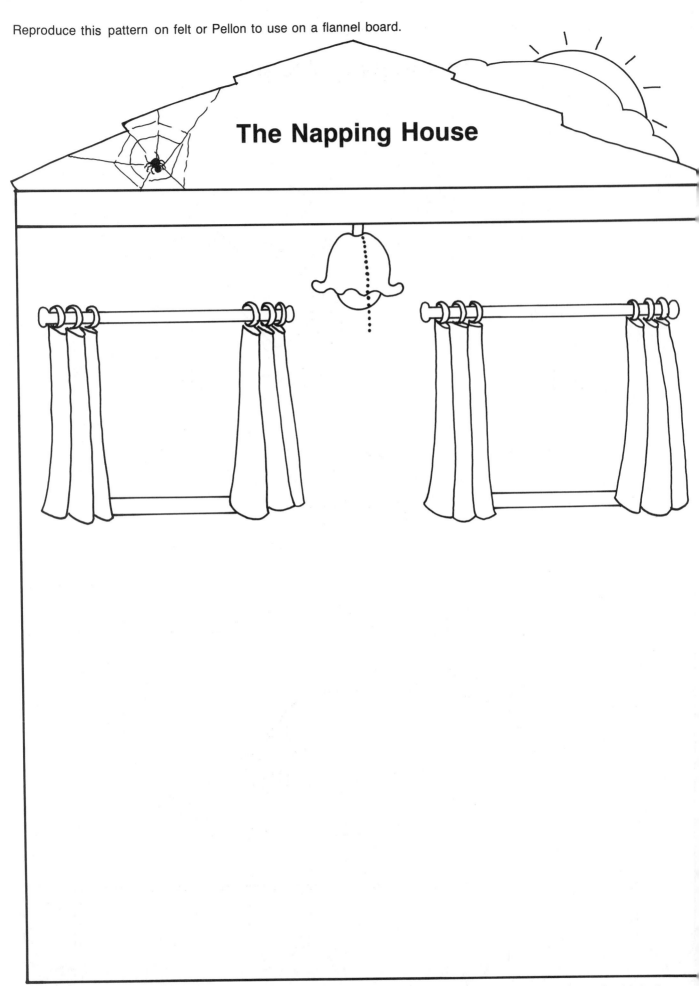

The Napping House

Read It Again

The Tale of Peter Rabbit
by Beatrix Potter
Frederick Warne 1908

1 READ

Read *The Tale of Peter Rabbit* for fun.

2 READ IT AGAIN

Read *The Tale of Peter Rabbit.*

- Ask questions such as these:
    Can you name all of the little rabbits in the story?
    How did Peter disobey his mother?
    What did Mr. McGregor do when he saw Peter?
    How did Peter get away?
    Have you ever done something your mother told you not to do? What happened?

- Real or Make-believe?

  Have your students explain which events in the story could really happen to a rabbit and which could not happen. If this is too difficult for your group, help by asking questions such as:
    Do real rabbits wear clothes?
    Can a rabbit live in a hole in the ground?
    Do rabbits eat plants?
    Does a mother rabbit feed her children bread and milk?

- Science Time

  If possible, bring a real rabbit into the classroom for children to see up close. (Remind them that they must be very gentle and quiet or they will frighten the rabbit.) Discuss what a real rabbit looks like. Have students list other animals that have fur, four legs, etc. Introduce the term mammals to older students.

  Have children find pictures of other animals with fur (mammals) in magazines. Let each child share his picture with the group. Glue the pictures to a chart and write each animal's name by the picture. This becomes the start of an animal "pictionary" to refer to later.

Read *The Tale of Peter Rabbit.*

Practice math readiness skills using the patterns on pages 31 and 44. Select one or two activities to do at a time. Don't try to do all of the suggestions in one period of time.

• Patterning — Reproduce the rabbits on page 31 on construction paper in several colors. Place several rabbits in a row creating a pattern. Begin with short, simple patterns. Provide a longer, more complex pattern as children become more experienced.

Select one or more children to copy the pattern.

Select one or more children to continue the pattern.

Have older, more able students try to create the pattern in reverse order.

Show the pattern, remove it, and have children try to recreate it from memory.

• Reproduce the jacket and button patterns on page 44. (Use felt if you wish to do this activity on a flannel board. Otherwise, cut them from construction paper.) Place the jacket on a flannel board or on a table.

Place several buttons on the jacket. Ask the children to tell you how many buttons are on Peter's jacket. Repeat several times.

Ask a child to place a given number of buttons on the jacket. Have the remaining children count the buttons to see if the number is correct.

Practice "one less." Place several buttons on the jacket. Ask children to tell you how many buttons will be left if you take one away. Remove one button and have them count to see if their guess was correct. (You can practice "one more" using the same materials.)

• Make a simple graph. Give each child one rabbit. (Use the pattern on page 31.) Make a large chart with "yes" and "no" at the bottom. Ask the question "Do you have a toy rabbit?" Have each child answer and place the rabbit pattern in the correct row.

READ IT AGAIN

Read *The Tale of Peter Rabbit.*

- In Mr. McGregor's Garden

Have children recall which vegetables were growing in Mr. McGregor's garden. (Use the illustrations if they have difficulty remembering.) Then have them see how many other vegetables they can name.

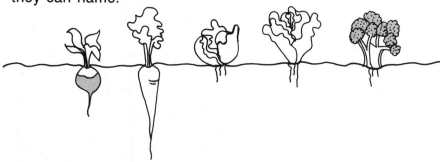

- "Tasting Day"

Bring samples of the types of vegetables in Mr. McGregor's garden. Encourage children to sample each of the vegetables. Discuss how the vegetables look and how they taste. Tally how many children like and dislike each of the vegetables.

- "What is in my basket?"

Use a real basket and real vegetables if possible. If not, cut out a basket shape from construction paper and use pictures of vegetables from magazines.

Show each vegetable. Have children name and describe it, and tell one way it can be eaten.

Name a vegetable (or ask a riddle about it) and select a child to pick it out of the basket and put it on the table. You can continue play when the basket is empty by having children find the correct vegetable and put it back into the basket.

Note: Reproduce the jacket on blue felt and the buttons on yellow or gold felt. (Or use blue and yellow construction paper.)

Peter's Jacket

> ## The Very Busy Spider
> ### by Eric Carle
> ### Philomel Books 1984

READ

Read *The Very Busy Spider* for fun. Take time for each child to feel the spider web and the fly.

READ IT AGAIN

Read *The Very Busy Spider.*

- Ask questions such as these:
  - What was the spider doing?
  - What does a spider use to make its web?
  - Why was the spider making a web?
  - Why didn't the spider speak to any of the animals?
  - What did the spider catch to eat?
  - What else do you think a spider might catch in its web for dinner?

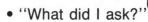

- "What did I ask?"
  Show the illustrations of the animals one at a time. Begin the sentence and see if the children can recall what that animal asked the spider. (Provide the answer yourself if the children have difficulty.) For example:

  "Neigh! Neigh!" said the horse. "Want to _____?"
  (answer — go for a ride)

  Create original sentences following the same format. For example:

  "Buzz! Buzz!" said the bee. "Want to eat my honey?"
  "Growl! Growl!" said the bear. "Want to fish with me?"

  Older students can dictate their sentences for you to write down. Let them illustrate their own sentences. Then staple the pages together to create a class book.

3
READ IT AGAIN

Read *The Very Busy Spider.*

- Show the illustrations again. Have children find the fly on each page.

- Science Time

  Have the children look at the picture of the spider carefully. Ask "What can you tell me about a spider?" If children have difficulty coming up with answers, guide them with questions such as "How many legs does it have?" or "What does a spider use its silk thread for?"

  If you have older students, create a class report about spiders by making a chart of the information they share. Put the chart up in the classroom along with other picture books about spiders.

> Spiders
> Spiders have 8 legs.
>
> Spiders spin webs.

Have the children look at the pictures of the fly carefully. Have them count the legs, wings and body parts. Ask "How are the spider and the fly different?" If they have difficulty, guide them with questions such as "How many legs does the fly have? How many legs does the spider have? Which one has the most legs?"

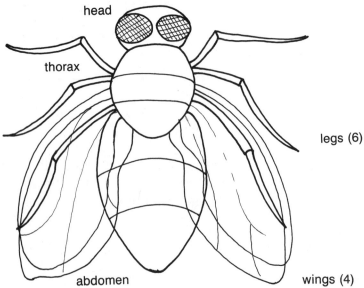

head

thorax

legs (6)

abdomen

wings (4)

Read *The Very Busy Spider.*

4

READ IT AGAIN

- Use the illustrations to practice descriptive language.
Show each farm animal. Have the children name its color, tell how many legs it has, and describe any special features. You may need to help children with the correct word to use for parts such as hooves, mane, horns, snout, wool, etc. Encourage children to use terms such as soft, fluffy, sharp, pointed, dark, light, tall, long, etc.

- This story takes place on a farm. Ask your students to see how many farm animals they can name. Then have them see if they can:
  Tell one fact about the animal.
  Make the animal's sound.
  Move in the same way the animal moves.

- Teach your children how to sing "Old MacDonald had a Farm."

- Teach your class how to play "The Farmer in the Dell."

Other Activities

Explore Textures — Use this book to begin a discussion of how things feel. Allow children to feel the spider's web again. Then have them feel their own clothing to see what other textures they feel. You will probably need to help them with words that clearly describe the feeling of each item (smooth, rough, soft, slick, bumpy, scratchy, etc.).

Collect items with interesting textures. For example:

wool	silk	velvet	corduroy
leather	flannel	sandpaper	waxed paper
oilcloth	plastic	cotton balls	rocks
netting	bark	styrofoam	dried flowers

Let children explore the different items and discuss how they feel. When they are familiar with the items, ask them to find specific textures for you. For example: "Show me something that feels soft."

Make a "Feely" box activity. Take two boxes. Put samples of fabric in each box. (Be sure each box contains one sample of each fabric.) Have a child close his or her eyes and try to match fabric by how it feels.

Art — Make spiders and spider webs.

- Spiders:

  Make the bodies of the spiders from modeling clay. Use pieces of pipe cleaner for the eight legs.

  > Roll clay into a ball.
  > Pinch one side to form a head.
  > Make a bend in each piece of pipe cleaner.
  > Stick four pipe cleaners on each side of the spider's body.
  > Make a face by poking with the tip of a pencil.

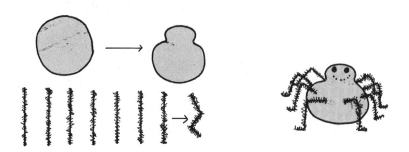

- Webs:

  Use white glue to form webs that have texture. Provide small squeeze bottles of glue and sheets of dark blue or black construction paper. Let children squeeze out the shape of a spider web onto the paper. Allow the glue to dry thoroughly. Older children may want to add a "very busy spider" made from construction paper to the web. (If you want the spider webs to sparkle, let children sprinkle their "webs" with silver glitter while the glue is still wet.)

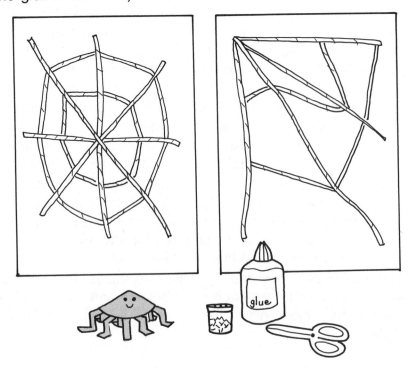

   Read It Again